T0156717

HOW TO SELL
YOU
...AND YOUR PRODUCT, SERVICE, OR IDEA

HOW TO SELL
YOU
...AND YOUR PRODUCT, SERVICE, OR IDEA

GLORIA WADSWORTH

iUniverse, Inc.
New York   Bloomington

How to Sell YOU...and Your Product, Service, or Idea

Copyright © 2010 Speaking Essentials INC

All rights reserved. No part of this book may be used or reproduced by any means, graphic, electronic, or mechanical, including photocopying, recording, taping or by any information storage retrieval system without the written permission of the publisher except in the case of brief quotations embodied in critical articles and reviews.

iUniverse books may be ordered through booksellers or by contacting:

iUniverse
1663 Liberty Drive
Bloomington, IN 47403
www.iuniverse.com
1-800-Authors (1-800-288-4677)

Because of the dynamic nature of the Internet, any Web addresses or links contained in this book may have changed since publication and may no longer be valid. The views expressed in this work are solely those of the author and do not necessarily reflect the views of the publisher, and the publisher hereby disclaims any responsibility for them.

ISBN: 978-1-4502-2484-0 (sc)
ISBN: 978-1-4502-2485-7 (ebk)

Library of Congress Control Number: 2010906383

Printed in the United States of America

iUniverse rev. date: 06/07/2010

Dedication

This book is dedicated to the memory of my mother, Catherine Wadsworth, who taught me about God through her love, faith, and hope for me. Because of her absolute support and unselfish sacrifices, I continue to enjoy opportunities that yield success and enable me to seek my full potential. To God, I am grateful for the gift of my mom and her loving spirit that will be with me through eternity.

"And now these three remain: faith, hope, and love. But the greatest of these is love"
1 Corinthians 13:13

Acknowledgments

My sincerest appreciation and gratitude to the following individuals for sharing the journey with me:

Gregory T Wadsworth, for your partnering with me on daily scriptural readings, and for your feedback on the book review.

Marian Pierce, for your enduring friendship that always avails a lifeline for me in time of need, for reviewing the book from your creatively gifted perspective and providing honest feedback.

Deborah "Debbie" Burnett, for God bringing us together at the right time in the right place, for reviewing the book, providing feedback with such "fine points", and for inspiring me through your loving spirit.

Andrew Morrison, for introducing me to the "16 Week Challenge". Our West Coast Group, through your vision, met weekly, setting challenges and sharing best practices. Research for this book was set and met during some of those "16 Week Challenge" sessions. Thank you to our team: Deanna Palmer, Brother Adrian Hickman, Sallie Craig, Kim Ransom

Demetria Bennett, for all your support and belief in the vision

L. R. Giles, for your commitment, critique, and collaboration on this project. Your editorial comments provided valuable feedback and I look forward to continuing the journey with you for the next book.

Table of Contents

Introduction 1
The Secret Ingredient to Selling 3
Introducing the Five Steps to Successful Selling 7
  The Associated 5 W's 8
Step #1: Start With YOU! 9
  First Impression 10
  Exuberate Confidence 11
  Build the Relationship 13
  Personal Appearance 20
    Recommended Attire for Women: 21
    Recommended Attire for Men: 22
    Unacceptable Business Casual Attire: 22
  4.0 Goal Winning Attitude (GWA) 23
    Positive Attitude 23
    Professional Attitude .25
    Persistent Attitude 26
    Patient Attitude 26
  Effective Communications 27
    Demonstrate Great Listening Skills 30
    Dos and Don'ts in Listening 32
  Be YOU! 33
Step #2: Engage in Dialogue 35
Step #3: Understand the Customer's Needs 43
Step #4: Position Your Solution 51
  "How to Say It" Tactics 56
Objections 59
Step #5: The Close 63
  Closing Techniques 63
  Action Plan 68
It Starts with You Poem 69
A Day on Selling Something Street 71
About the Author 73

Introduction

Do you remember your first boyfriend or girlfriend? What about the first time you tried out for the basketball or cheerleader team? How about the time you talked the Highway Officer out of giving you that traffic ticket?

Let me take you down memory lane, if I may. I am driving a silver two-seater automobile in Atlanta, Georgia on a sunny day. Actually, I am speeding in this sports car. I hear a siren, and see blue flashing lights in my rearview mirror. When I pull over to the side of the road, a very determined-to-give-me-a-ticket Highway Patrolman approaches me.

As he began to PUSH me through the process of giving me a speeding ticket, I began to PULL him through the process of NOT giving me one.

He asks me questions, and I pull out my asthma medicine to fake an asthma attack. The patrolman then tells me he could arrest me for driving under the influence of drugs. I tell him I work for IBM in Human Resources and might get fired if I am arrested or get a traffic ticket.

"I have to give you a ticket," he says. I beg to be let off with just a warning. Yet, the officer proceeds to write the ticket. As the officer finishes writing the ticket and redirects his eyes on me, I manage to workup one life-saving teardrop in my eye. Feeling a little frightened and meek I open my eyes as wide as I can, gazing my watery, but sparkling pupils directly into the officer's eyes. Speaking softly, I humbly plead my case, begging the officer to issue me a warning ticket. After a moment of silence, the highway patrolman looks at me and asks, "What did you say you do for IBM?"

I replied, "I work in Human Resources."

The officer says, "Well, you should be in sales because you just sold me on a warning ticket."

I begin shouting, "Thank you, thank you, Jesus!!"

I share this story with you to say you never know who you might have to sell to. You might have to sell to the Highway Patrolman or a local community group. You might have to sell to the executive on Wall Street or your neighbor on Main Street. You might to have to sell to your mother, your father, your brother, your sister, your teacher, your preacher, your husband, your wife, your enemy, your friend, your child, your school, your church, or your employer. Regardless of who you have to sell to, the secret to the process is this: It all starts with YOU!

The secret ingredient to selling is YOU!

In this book, *How to Sell YOU…and Your Product, Service, or Idea* I share some critical information on selling as well as some tactical and strategic examples of the process.

The Secret Ingredient to Selling

If you sell products or services for a living and you're reading this book, you are going to discover the secret ingredient to selling is not your product or service, IT'S YOU! If you are reading this book and do not sell a product or service for a living, you are going to discover that you are a salesperson, too! The secret ingredient you sell everyday is YOU!

When I was 15, myself along with two other top students in the sophomore class, were selected to interview with IBM for a high school work program. While I maintained an honor student status and enjoyed learning, I also believed in balance and having fun. People skills were natural for me as I grew up in a community where our family home was "home to the community". On the day of the interview, while the other students appeared nervous, I was very excited about the opportunity to speak with the interviewer regarding the IBM position. I was glad to speak with someone outside of my learning institution. To me, speaking with the IBM manager was learning in itself.

When the IBM representative arrived to interview me and the other students, the teacher approached me and said, "Gloria, he wants to see you now."

My inner voice whispered to my ears, "And I want to see him because I am ready for this."

I was so ready to start talking with this interviewer.

In the interview room, I introduced myself and the interview proceeded. I spoke about my family and how my parents had divorced. I talked about the impact the divorce had on my education and aspirations, but how the inspiration from my mother encouraged me to overcome the odds. I spoke of how my mother taught me to know the strength of my roots and build from my origin to be the best I could be. And from those roots, I have been driven to succeed.

I think I told that man my life story. I felt very comfortable speaking with this IBM manager who I did not even know. And to my pleasure, I was selected to the program. The interviewer commented, "With your personality, you can go far in life."

Why did IBM choose me? I did not sell this interviewer on my grade point average because I did not have the highest grade point average (GPA) among those interviewed. Nor did I sell the interviewer on my attendance record, because I was not a student who sought a perfect attendance certificate at the year-end school awards assembly. When my friends suggested cutting class and going to the lake for fun, I'd go and not think twice about it. Remember, I believed in balance!

What I sold during that interview was ME! And as you read the following chapters of this book, you will gain critical insights into this first step of the selling process, **Step #1: Start with YOU!** Remember, the secret ingredient in selling is YOU!

You often hear two things in life are certain: death and taxes. What happens between birth and death is a result of our choices. The choices we make shape our future. The choices YOU make in the process of selling your product, service, or idea shape the result. The results yield a win or the results yield a loss. Remember... the sale Starts with YOU and Ends with YOU!

Whatever the situation or whomever the audience, know that selling is not just something some people do for a living, selling is a way of life for everyone! Yes, everyone. You are all salespeople, whether you know it or not.

Selling yourself is the secret ingredient that opens the doors of opportunity. Selling yourself is an approach that makes YOU a winner at this game. Throughout this book you will learn the fundamentals of this secret ingredient, Selling YOU!

Introducing the Five Steps to Successful Selling

Aside from being one of my favorite topics, selling is one of the oldest professions. It dates as far back as Adam and Eve. Remember, Eve sold Adam on biting that apple. Can you believe it? Eve is the oldest salesperson in the history of selling. It all started with Eve selling herself to Adam. That's **Step #1: Start with YOU.**

Unfortunately, all sales are not that simple. But, if you approach selling with a winning attitude that starts with you, you will succeed. And of course, the other side to this equation is who are you selling to and why do they want it? At times, what a person thinks they need is not what they need. It is critical to understand "the why". Why are you here? Why does the customer have a need?

In selling you want to really, really get to know your customer, their environment, their challenges, their threats, their strengths as well as short and long term objectives. Here is where we transition to **Step #2: Engage in Dialogue.**

John L. Graham, award-winning scholar and world recognized expert on international business negotiations, reminds us, "It is not what you want to sell when you want to sell it that matters today. It's what the customer wants to buy when the customer wants to buy it that counts."

While starting with you is the initial approach to selling, you must Engage in Dialogue to identify information about the customer, it is critical that you accurately identify what the customer needs. That's **Step #3: Understand the Customer's Needs.**

Once you have effectively engaged in dialogue to better understand your customer's environment, verified your customer's needs, and qualified your customer, it's time to smoothly transition to **Step #4: Position Your Solution.**

And **Step #5: The Close** is when you bring it all home and make it happen, secure the deal, and win the business!!! And let me say this, when you effectively execute steps 1 - 4, you are on cruise control as **Step #5: The Close** becomes automatic.

In David Mamet's film *Glengarry Glenross* Alec Baldwin portrays a consultant who introduces the ABC concept of sales. ABC stands for Always-Be-Closing. In other words, always gain customer agreement throughout the entire selling cycle and The Close becomes automatic.

The remainder of this book will further explore these five steps to successful selling while sharing stories that illustrate the process, step-by-step.

The Associated 5 W's

For each of the five steps to successful selling is an associated W: who, why, what, where, when.

- **Step #1: It Starts with YOU**. This is the "who".
- **Step #2: Engage in Dialogue**. This is the "why". Why are you here? Why does the customer have a need?
- **Step #3: Understand Customer Needs**. This is the "what". What does the customer need or desire?
- **Step #4: Position Your Solution**. This is the "where". Where you lay out your plan, product, service or idea.
- And last but not least, the moment we've all celebrated in sales, **Step #5: The Close**. This is the "when", when you win the business.

Step #1: Start With YOU!

Step number one is your time to shine, It Starts with YOU. Whitney Houston sings "give me one moment in time" and Step #1 is *your* moment in time. It Starts with YOU; it's your time to shine. If you really want to succeed at selling, you must sell yourself first.

So often we are so busy presenting our services or products, we fail to engage the customer, to uncover their needs and interest, to understand who they really are, what they really want, and why they really want it. Question: what are you really selling? Is it a product, an opportunity, a service? Or is it a vision, a dream, an idea?

What you might think you are selling is not what you are really selling. You are selling YOU. Ask any athlete who did not make the NBA draft, but later made a professional team as a walk-on candidate. Ask any student who was not accepted into college based on academic credentials. Ask any employee who was not promoted solely based on an excellent performance record. Each of the above statements demonstrates the secret ingredient to success in selling is YOU, not the technical qualifications, not an academic record. So how do we sell YOU? Here are seven essentials:

- ➤ First Impression
- ➤ Exuberate Confidence
- ➤ Build the Relationship

➤ Personal Appearance
➤ Goal Winning Attitude
➤ Effective Communications
➤ Be You

First Impression

We all know that a first impression is instant and everlasting. So what can you do to make a positive one? You can smile. You want to smile like you have been paid to, and believe me you will be paid.

Research shows 72% of people who smile are considered confident. And 86% of people say they are more likely to strike up a conversation with a stranger who smiles.

Dale Carnegie says in his book *How to Win Friends and Influence People*, "A smile costs nothing, but creates much." So smile and create a great first impression. Smile and create an interest in your product. Smile and create a "yes" in your customer's mind. Treat your customers with respect and smile, even when they don't smile back. Smiling is contagious and eventually they will smile, even if it is a "silent smile" as seen through one's eyes.

A smile can positively impact your bottom line. Your objective in the first step of selling is to make a great impression and smiling sets you off to a great start.

Once when I performed as a professional dancer at the Ford Theatre in Los Angeles, a lady whose daughter was a member of our dance group came from the audience and said, "You smile like you really enjoy what you do and I really enjoyed your performance!"

I graciously responded, "I do." I totally enjoyed performing! And smiling made it that much better. A smile has a powerful impact and can move audiences!

A smile radiates warmth and hides problems, and we are supposed to be problem solvers for our customers, not problem creators.

Someone once said, "A smile happens in a flash, but its memory lasts a lifetime." Smiling is a basic foundation for excellent customer service. And great customer service is what differentiates customers from competitors. So smile and make a great first impression!

Exuberate Confidence

Exuberating confidence might start with a firm handshake and good eye contact during an initial meeting with the customer. For example, most people you call on to sell a product are usually very knowledgeable in their respective area of expertise. So when you greet them for the first time, their confidence shows. And because you are an expert in your area, your confidence should show as well.

In presenting yourself as a consultant or an expert to your customer, one way to demonstrate confidence in your delivery is through eye contact. If you're hesitant to sell, the customer is going to be hesitant to buy or agree with any of your recommendations. For example, when speaking with the customer about your product or service, you want to project strongly, demonstrating your belief in your product. If you show any doubt in the capability of your product, the customer will have doubts in your product. For example, if you are selling a cell phone, sell the phone's positives. Never speak to any of your product's weaknesses. You must always positively represent your product and company with confidence. Be confident enough to demonstrate your product. I have seen sales representatives that were afraid to demonstrate the product, thinking it may self destruct during the demo process. When you demonstrate your product with confidence, you recommend your solution through the ABC technique, Always Be Closing.

When we talk about eye contact, please look at the customer and not at your notes. Your talk should be one of consultation, and not memorization. You want to look at the customer and not at the customer's wall or desk when you speak. During this stage of selling YOU, as the focus will be on YOU, gain confidence by connecting with the customer through direct eye contact.

Let me use a scenario to emphasize the impact of eye contact. When I was with IBM Corporation's Human Resources Department,

I was involved in a program at the Los Angeles Urban League Training Center in which a very prominent syndicated news show was considering taping a story about the program. The news show invited six managers from IBM including myself to attend an Executive Television Workshop in preparation for this interview about the program.

During that workshop, we saw a video on the importance of eye contact during an interview. This particular news show filmed individuals from the neck up, so facial gestures would clearly be revealed on the big screen.

Knowing this, we were advised not to look directly into the camera. We could look down briefly at our notes, BUT NEVER LOOK UP. If we looked up, it would appear as though we were trying to "catch a fly off the wall". Have someone take a photo of you looking up during a talk, and you will get the picture. When meeting with clients, same rule applies. If you are not able to look directly into a person's eyes, look down briefly, but never look up. Direct eye contact demonstrates confidence and confidence sells YOU!

In sales, never avoid eye contact. When you avoid eye contact, you avoid the sale. When you avoid eye contact, you lose confidence and credibility. When you avoid eye contact, you lose an opportunity to sell 90% of you. When a person looks at you, your eyes represent 90% of what they see. Your eyes communicate silently to the person you are speaking to. Direct eye contact is a way to increase trust through nonverbal body language. People feel if you cannot look at them, they cannot—and will not—trust you.

Don't read your notes. Quickly scan your notes and then speak clearly and fluently. Always make direct eye contact regardless if you are speaking to an audience of one or one thousand. Let your voice speak from consultation, not memorization. Demonstrate confidence!

A firm handshake can say as much about your confidence as your appearance. I've had people give me a weak handshake, and the little voice inside me would say, "This is going to be an uphill battle."

But, like Les Brown says, "They might knock you down, but if you can look up, you can get up." And I did, mentally. Remember, exuberate confidence in selling!

I've also had people squeeze the life out of my little hand in an effort to intimidate me. But I would squeeze right back, demonstrating my power, my passion, and my purpose. My purpose was to sell; I was passionate about my product and felt very powerful in the moment.

After all Shakespeare says, "All the world's a stage and men and women merely players." So I would enter a room, psyche myself into believing that I was on stage, exuberating confidence in my delivery every time....Starting with Me!

Always demonstrate confidence with direct eye contact and a firm handshake. Earn the right to advance. Remember, Start with YOU... is the cue!

Build the Relationship

In this first stage of the selling process you begin to build the relationship, the foundation for partnering with a customer or connecting with an individual. If you can close the customer on a relationship, you can close the customer on a sale! And you know what they say, "It is not the storm that tears down buildings, it is the foundation." Start building the foundation, the relationship!

Let me share a story. One of my key clients, Mr. David Maxey, Trainer for an aerospace company, ordered some training materials for an upcoming class and my warehouse sent far less than the necessary quantity. Mr. Maxey called me in a state of panic because the class date was two days away. He needed his complete training material order for the class within one day. I immediately contacted my warehouse management and advised the training materials absolutely needed to be delivered same day or next day to Mr. David Maxey. The materials were being shipped from our warehouse distribution center in Chicago to the customer destination in Los Angeles. While the warehouse successfully delivered the materials the next day in time for Mr. Maxey's class, this rush caused him unnecessary distress.

Once the completed order was received, I received a phone call from Ms. Linda Oliver, Director of Training and Development. Ms. Oliver called to inquire about the mishap. Prior to contacting me, Ms. Oliver had a discussion with company trainers who were expecting the shipment of materials and had first notified her about the delay in shipment. Ms. Oliver and I discussed the problem as well as a solution. In addition, I informed Ms. Oliver of a quality check process my company was implementing to ensure timely delivery of materials shipped to their organization. At the end of our phone discussion, Ms. Oliver's final comment to me was, "I told them, not Gloria. She always provides the best customer service."

As you might conclude from this scenario, the area of focus was not about the delivery error of the training materials. The area of focus was not about the product. Ms. Oliver's area of focus was me and the relationship I had with her and her organization. Because of the relationship I had with my customer, my customer went to bat for me! Because of the relationship I had with my customer, I did not lose the business over a delivery error. Remember, Start with YOU…and build a relationship with your client.

Let me share another scenario. I had not heard from Ruby Bowman of Inacore Computers for a period of time. I knew from our relationship that Inacore Computers usually places an order for training materials during specific times of the year. I called Ms. Bowman, who usually places the order, leaving a voicemail inquiring why I had not received an order during February or June. I asked if it was due to any service issues, because at Speaking Essentials, we are committed to excellence in service. Ruby responded via email placing an order that same day, stating the organization had cut back on training, but was planning a class the following month.

When you have a client that you can contact on the spur of the moment, with no barriers between you, and inquire about getting business, you have a relationship. Whenever fear exists between your client and you, or whenever distrust exists, work needs to be done to remove such barriers.

Often times a customer will buy from you if they like you. A customer will like you if they trust you. A customer will trust you if they respect you. Establishing respect and trust is critical in building relationships. Trust stems from reliance and dependability. Respect stems from character and integrity. To establish trust with your client, you have to establish your dependability. For example, ensure a timely response to all correspondence and always provide the client with the information they request. To establish respect with your client, simply exercise truthfulness, politeness, and professionalism from start to finish.

This does not mean you'll always agree with a customer. On the other hand, you should never be untruthful with a customer or allow your emotions to result in rude or unprofessional behavior. Disagreements do not destroy the relationship; the lack of foundation destroys the relationship. You want to develop powerful relationships with your clients that result in the client liking you, trusting you, and respecting you even when they may disagree with you. You want to always work on building the relationship, not tearing it down. In building a relationship with a foundation on trust and respect, you will be able to connect with your client on a personal and professional level. Often you will win the business simply because they like YOU!

Reward your client by giving the best customer service possible. Studies show 80% of your business is likely to come from 20% of your customers. Acknowledge your loyal customers and always provide the best possible customer service. Constantly seek ways to improve your customer service.

Whenever your customer presents a problem to you, resolve it immediately. Research suggests customers gain a stronger affinity for sales representatives who respond to their issues immediately and completely.

When I was a representative for an organization selling personal computers to technology dealers, I received a call that a client was looking for a networking product used to link numerous computers. I quickly polled my dealership base, thinking this is an easy fix. However, I was unable to locate the product through my usual channels. I had to quickly act on alternative options as I did not want the customer to go to the competition. I polled my peers throughout the Southern California Region, once again, to no avail. Finally, I was informed this specific networking product was in very limited distribution at the time. Rather than tell my customer, "I am sorry, but we are unable to obtain the product, due to constraints," I did further research to identify when the products would be available. Through that additional research, I identified a computer dealer who was willing to sell his entire shipment of the networking products to my customer.

While this was a challenge because this product was in limited supply and most of the dealers had backorders to fill, I was able to resolve the customer's issue completely and in a timely manner. To my customer, this represented excellent service.

In addition to providing excellent service when building relationships, reward your loyal customers with incentives. As buyers, we like incentives we get through frequent flyer programs, credit card discount allowances, retail coupons, and more! Our customers want and need to know you appreciate and value their business. Customers, who spend the most *with* me, get the most *from* me in terms of rewards. I once heard a speaker say because her youngest child always went to the supermarket with her, her youngest child always got the items she wanted. Whereas the older kids did not want to go, yet, would always ask, "Why didn't she buy this product or that product?"

I always reward my highest revenue generating clients with an incentive, whether it is tangible or intangible. Let your customers know you truly appreciate and value them. Reward your customers and continue to strengthen the relationship.

People today are more customer-focused, not product-focused. People want the service, the relationship. Start rewarding your loyal customers. Expand your service, give incentives, focus on your customer more, and build the relationship! So when the storm comes—and storms will come—the relationship you have with your customer will weather the storm.

Just as personal relationships are not created in a day, week, or month, professional relationships are not created in a day, week, or month. Can you imagine starting a relationship and getting married all in a month or less? Yes, it could work short-term, but because you do not really know one another, it probably will not work long-term.

On the contrary, if you do it right and *build a relationship* first, you have a much better chance at making it work. What I am saying is the more effort you put into first building a relationship with your customer, the more business or cooperation you will get from your customer long-term. Investment in the relationship will yield increase from the relationship.

Give your customer reasons to trust you. Demonstrate to your customer reasons to respect you. Invest in the time to nurture the relationship so that the foundation is strong. Show genuine interest in your customer and your customer's needs. Always treat your customer with respect.

Validate your customer's trustworthiness as well. Ensure they are upfront with you. If they say they are the decision maker, make sure they are! It takes two to maintain a successful relationship! And everyone's time is valuable, including yours!

Can you remember how many times you walked into a store and instantly purchased a TV, computer, luggage, or any item with the salesperson presenting the item, but not selling you the item? And how many of those salespeople do you remember? My guess is none.

On the other hand, how many times do you walk into a store and spend some time engaging in dialogue with the sales representative before you make a decision to buy the item? And how many of these salespeople do you remember? My guess is many of them. In fact, some of them you will never forget.

You will always remember the person who sold you an item when the person took time to understand you, what you need, and why you need it.

When I visit Macy's in New York City, I always seek out their shoes! I instinctively look for the sale items first. Because I have frequented Macy's shoe department over the years, I have built a relationship with one of Macy's top shoe salespeople, Leon Adkins. Leon impressed me the first time we met by taking time to understand me, what I needed, and why I needed it.

In establishing rapport through small talk, Leon got the sale. Now, every time I visit Macy's in New York Leon meets me, gives me a warm greeting, and starts the small talk while identifying my needs. He gives me up to date information on the New York Yankees and game day weather forecast because he knows I am a diehard fan and will likely attend a game during my stay. After engaging in small talk and understanding my needs, Leon positions a display of shoes in front of me, and leaves me alone. Because of the relationship I developed with Leon during my visits to Macy's, he knows exactly how to service me. And more often than not, I will buy multiple pairs of shoes.

The key point: Leon Adkins started with the *who* and sold me on who he was through a great first impression, and a very professional, positive attitude. He got to know *who* I was, what I wanted, and why I really wanted it. Because he invested time to build a relationship, not to push the sale on me, he won the business that day and I was very happy with the product I purchased. Leon demonstrated why he was a top salesperson at Macy's store in New York City. Leon Adkins invests a lot of time and patience in building the relationship and creating a win/win situation with his customers.

The 21st Century customer wants quality, performance, price, and relationship. Today's customers have lots of choices…and they know it. They demand it all, and can have it all. And while quality, performance, and price might appear as a commodity, relationship will never be a commodity. I don't know about you, but I consider myself priceless and will never be a commodity. Relationships are built to last on the intangibles, not tangibles.

Often relationships are started through referrals or "who you know". Once I had a very difficult time getting a meeting with the President of a nonprofit organization. Yet, my assignment included building a relationship with this customer to position my organization for future partnering opportunities. Most nonprofit establishments are only concerned with its customers, its donors, and its volunteers. After numerous attempts to contact the President of the nonprofit establishment, Mr. Michael Sulton, I finally put together a smart strategy. I received information that Mr. Sulton was to be honored at an awards event, so I purchased a ticket to attend same event.

The event's setting was very elegant and hospitable. Delightful sounds of the harp filled the air. Dressed in black tie attire, everyone appeared to be at their best game. Of course, I am thinking this is the moment in time, my time to shine. My only goal that evening was to meet Mr. Sulton and build rapport for future opportunities with his nonprofit organization. Not knowing hundreds of people would fill the room, I was not able to locate Mr. Sulton during the reception.

As the awards program started and dinner was served, the announcer began to acknowledge special guests in attendance. Fortunately, the key guest to be honored was Mr. Sulton, and he was sitting at the table directly behind me. Shortly after Mr. Sulton was acknowledged, I walked over to his table and briefly introduced myself. I complimented him on a presentation he'd given previously at a church service I attended. Leveraging the relationship with Mr. Sulton's church gave me credibility.

He said, "The pastor of that church is one of my favorite people whom I respect tremendously."

That was my green light, time to go for it. I said, "Well, we always enjoy your visits to the church. Your church, ZionWay, is one of my accounts and I have been trying to get an appointment, but have not had any luck."

He said, "Call my associate, here is his card and tell him I sent you."

In addition, Mr. Sulton introduced me to his assistant who sat next to him. His assistant told me to call him the following day for an appointment as well.

By the time I finished engaging in dialogue, not only did I begin to build the relationship, but I received a commitment for an appointment.

Incidentally, attending an awards event to get in the door with a customer is certainly a way to differentiate yourself from the competition. Specificity versus generalities gives you a competitive edge. In building a quality relationship with your clients, differentiate yourself from competition. Let me say this about competition: never be threatened by it. I don't know about you, but I will differentiate myself and beat all of my competitors through selling me. Not my product. Not my price. Me. I love competition. How can you be at the top if there is no one under you?

Know your competition, know your industry, know your product, and know your customer. Remember, we are in a knowledge-based environment. Use the knowledge in building the relationship and Selling YOU!

With attention to the few customers who refuse to speak with you *at any time*, you might want to keep their name on your Mail Only list. Send a Christmas card, sample product, or industry literature to stay in touch. Eventually the customer may stop objecting to your calls, speak with you, and began to build the relationship.

Personal Appearance

Do looks really matter? Yes. Absolutely, as 93 percent of all communication is nonverbal. Personal appearance counts! At times your visual appearance can distract from or distort your presentation.

Your personal appearance, your image, your wardrobe are all key to the first 30 seconds of an introduction. Your audience is going to hear you by what you wear.

Let me share a story with you. I went to my doctor's new office and this well-dressed, very young man—slightly more than three feet tall—approached me holding a briefcase. He extended a firm handshake, and very professionally introduced himself. He demonstrated the utmost confidence and proceeded to ask how he might help me. I was very impressed with him, but thought he looked awfully young to be doing this job.

I later found out he was the doctor's son, playing doctor. But this young man's appearance—suit, dress shirt, tie, and briefcase—was so professional, he had the patients, including myself, fooled. Yes, appearance counts!

You want to always look good, and you should always dress at least as formally as the people with whom you will be meeting. Know that conservative dress is always safe.

If you are going to speak at a church, dress like you are going to church. If you are going to hang out with golfers, dress like golfers. If you are going to lunch with executives, dress like an executive.

If your audience is Business Formal, conservative dress is suggested. Never underestimate the power of a navy blue suit and white top. If your audience is Business Casual, I have some guidelines for you.

Recommended Attire for Women:

- Pantsuits or skirts
- Classic Sheath paired with a sweater or blazer in the same color and fabric
- White shirts added to dress pants, khakis, or skirts
- Closed-toe shoes (hosiery is not essential for Business Casual, but is recommended when wearing shorter skirts)
- While jewelry, scarves, and other accessories complement the wardrobe, always remember; less is best when it comes to accessories.

Recommended Attire for Men:

- A sports coat without tie, dark pants, or khakis
- Traditional dress slack khakis, Dockers, corduroys, wool flannel and linen slacks with blazer
- Casual button-down oxford shirts without a tie
- Oxfords and loafers in brown or black

Unacceptable Business Casual Attire:

- Jeans or denim pants, shorts
- Leggings, stretch pants, pants with stirrup, sweat pants, spandex or other form fitting pants
- Athletic shoes, hiking boots, sandals, or flip flops
- Flannel shirts or t-shirts
- Hats/Caps

Remember the first impression is paramount, so dress appropriately. Dress for success! Henry Ward Beecher, one of the greatest orators of his time, said, "Clothes and manners do not make the man; but, when he is made, they greatly improve his appearance." Dress to impress and your impression will determine your success.

In Marketing one of the most important attributes of a product is packaging. Companies spend millions of dollars packaging their products to attract customers. And it works! Think about the items you put in your cart at the supermarket simply based on the packaging. Think about how much money you spend on Christmas gifts based on the way they are packaged versus the contents. And how often do we buy shoes based on how they look rather than how they feel? Oh, let's not forget our attraction to another human being. Is it based purely on the outside, the packaging?

Your personal appearance is *your* packaging. When I was a Sales Representative for a Fortune 100 company and we wore our navy suits and white shirts, it signified class, culture, and credibility to our customers and business partners. It's the visual appeal that arouses interest from the start. Personal appearance counts and starts with YOU!

You want to look and feel good when selling you. Do you have a calm but cheerful look? Or did you rush in the room out of breath because you were running late? Always appear in control, even when circumstances make you feel out of control.

You want to look and feel good. Yes, you want to feel like a million dollars inside so you can visualize making a million dollars on the outside. Remember… personal appearance counts!

4.0 Goal Winning Attitude (GWA)

In selling, the right attitude can win the business and the wrong attitude can lose the business. Your goal is to maintain a *4.0 GWA, Goal Winning Attitude*. The 4.0 represents four points to describe your attitude: Positive, Professional, Persistent, and Patient. Let's explore them further.

Positive Attitude

I often hear sales representatives say, "I have challenges with Customer X."

My response, "Look into the mirror and see if the problem is external or internal."

Mr. Goethe, a German author, says, "Behavior is a mirror in which everyone displays his or her own image."

At times we may experience gridlock within ourselves. While our intentions are positive, internally we may experience negative energy that blocks the positive attitude. Negative energy is like a defective product. The actual performance of the product is not the expected or intended performance. For example, if I allowed a customer's negative energy to spill over into my space, regardless of my initial intentions, my behavior would become negative and not accomplish my objective for that particular meeting.

To win the relationship and to win the business, you must always maintain a positive attitude, even when the client is negative. I remember having to meet with a customer because other sales representatives were fearful and felt challenged with this client. I actually enjoyed meeting with Ms. Catherine Briggs, Managing Partner for one of the top accounting firms, because each time I met with Catherine, I knew I did not have any room to err. My number one goal with Ms. Briggs was to maintain a positive state of mind and execute ABC, Always Be Closing. A positive attitude will get you through customer objections and demonstrate your credibility and impressive character. Maintaining a positive attitude enabled me to maintain a healthy relationship with a difficult customer resulting in respect and revenue for my company.

Just like you feed your body food and water daily, your attitude needs to be fed positive and inspirational thoughts each day. Every day, I wake up and say, "This is the day the Lord has made, I WILL REJOICE AND BE GLAD IN IT!"

Because I consistently feed my mind inspiration and positive thoughts, even challenging days are good days.

Look into the mirror and ask yourself, "If I were a commodity or stock on Wall Street, would I invest in me?"

If you answer yes, proceed. If you answer no, then go back and do a "checkup from the neck up" as popular motivational speaker Zig Ziglar would say. Get a positive attitude and approach to proceed so that you will succeed. Your mind needs positive nourishment and encouragement on a regular basis.

You must plant positive seeds in your mind by reading self-help books to make you feel good about YOU. Nurture your mind with positive thoughts. Winston Churchill says, "A pessimist sees the difficulty in every opportunity; an optimist sees the opportunity in every difficulty."

Professional Attitude

Your *attitude*—not your *aptitude*— determines your *altitude* in life.

A professional attitude reflects specific attributes that include, but are not limited to: respect, commitment, excellence, leadership, and listening skills. We have to always remember when we are in front of the customer, to give our undivided attention through active listening. When we listen to our customers, we will see challenges as opportunities and will be able to proceed with the steps to win the business.

When we talk about attitude, we talk about how we feel and what we believe. When we talk about attitude, we express our values and act in certain ways. In selling, and specifically in selling YOU, it is essential that you maintain a professional attitude at all times, even when it's painful. Remember...no pain, no gain!

The biggest reason people fail in sales is the individual's attitude after hearing the word no. Les Brown always says, "When things go wrong, don't go with them."

As a positively professional person you anticipate and prepare for rejection. So when the customer yells at you with a no, maintain your state of calm and coolness. Collect your positive thoughts. Acknowledge the rejection. Answer the objection. Gain agreement and move into the next stage of your selling cycle.

For example, if you are trying to sell a car and the buyer is willing to pay $50,000, but your selling price is $55,000, do you collapse and walk away from the table? A salesperson with a nonchalant, order-taking attitude might. A professional salesperson with a consultative, order-maker attitude will communicate more to reach a mutually agreed upon price.

A salesperson who does not sit around waiting to take orders will do appropriate research and come back and close the deal with a cash offer of $53,000, plus some tangible or intangible gift, valued at $3,000. It's all in the professional attitude!!!

Persistent Attitude

Exercising a persistent attitude helps you view the objection as redirection to the goal. Another example is in football, when the ball is kicked to the receiving team, different possibilities may follow. Receiver A may run the ball from the 20 yard line to the 5 yard line, falling short of the goalpost, unable to score. Or, Receiver A might run the ball from the 20 yard line, then pass the ball to Receiver B from the 5 yard line. Receiver B then crosses the goal line, scoring a touchdown. The persistent and unselfish attitude of Receiver A created a win/win situation. Regardless of the challenges, stay focused on your objective while maintaining a persistent attitude to win.

Patient Attitude

Research shows that 80 percent of sales closed are made after the first sales call. Yet most sales representatives only follow up 10 percent of the time beyond the second call made to the customer. If I may offer a critical suggestion and key to successful selling, it is follow up and don't give up.

Remember, winners lose more than losers. Winners bounce back and play the game more. Winners are patient. In selling, patience must always be exercised. Patience is the capacity for calmly enduring painful, *trying situations.* As a salesperson you will always find yourself in *trying situations* simply because, until you actually gain the customer agreement, you are always *trying to* gain the customer agreement.

Success requires patience. Success endures challenges. Michelangelo demonstrated patience when he painted the Sistine Chapel. As he stated, "If people knew how hard I work to get my mastery, it wouldn't seem so wonderful at all."

Yet, we all know the beauty and success of the Sistine Chapel, one of the world's greatest works of art. Thomas Edison's patience led to the invention of the light bulb. After numerous attempts, failures, and never giving up, Edison successfully invented the light bulb.

When I was selling, as long as I maintained the relationship with a positive and patient attitude, I felt good about closing the sale. The key is the maintenance, which means staying in touch through emails, phone calls, holiday greetings, etc. The little things you do to maintain a relationship will strengthen the relationship. When you present a 4.0 Goal Winning Attitude, you always win. Sometimes your win may not happen when you want or expect it, but it will happen. Just hang with the process! Be positive. Be professional. Be patient. Be persistent.

In selling, the goal is to maintain a 4.0 Goal Winning Attitude, starting with YOU. Always exercise a positive, professional, persistent, and patient attitude throughout the process. The individual who succeeds in winning the sale is one that maintains a state of calm and a positive spirit. The individual who is a winner in the game of selling has a never give up attitude, even when the going gets rough.

A successful salesperson does not fear challenges, but sees objections as redirection towards the goal. As long as you are in the game with a winning attitude, you have an opportunity to win!

Effective Communications

Whether your first contact with a customer is verbal or nonverbal communication, it is absolutely essential that you communicate effectively. If the telephone is your medium, speak clearly and confidently. Be prepared when you call. AT&T says, "Reach out and touch someone," not just, "Reach out." Connect with the caller, relate to them.

Studies show 7 out of 10 business people lose their jobs because of poor communication skills. You can be cute, you can be nice, you can be neat, but if you do not communicate well with others about your business, idea, or offering, you will never sell successfully. Effective communications is essential to success!

To ensure effective communication consider role-playing prior to a meeting or presentation. When I practiced my sales presentations, I used my nine year old son. I had him sit at the end of the dining table as if he was an executive I was trying to sell to. I stressed that he was in charge. Of course, it made him feel special and important for a moment. To this day my son is very objective when he critiques my work, and I still benefit from his feedback.

By role-playing away from the customer, you are able to avoid uncomfortable situations in front of the customer. Role play allows you to eliminate any fears, build your confidence, and deliver your message with conviction.

Role play is an effective way to improve your communication skills through practice, feedback, and more practice. It's like writing a book. You never write a book without having it edited before publishing. In selling, always role play before communicating a critical message to your customer. Role play improves communications, increases confidence, and yields positive impact.

In fact role playing with my son not only improved my communication skills, but improved my son's communication skills as well. One year, my middle-school age son sold over 100 boxes of Christmas cards to neighbors in our community and made $300 in net profit leveraging the selling skills I demonstrated to him during our role play sessions. My neighbors would say, "You've created a junior sales executive that knows how to talk us out of our money!"

While in college my son received multiple job offers as a Civil Engineer Intern each summer. In fact one summer he received multiple job offers in a 24 hour period. What was my son telling those interviewers? He couldn't have been talking about his grades! Regardless of his academic prowess, he passed the test in selling himself! He learned how to communicate effectively through our role play exercises. Effective communications is essential to the success of any individual or organization!

While verbal communication is vital, sometimes nonverbal communication has the greater initial impact. When we think about first impression, it can happen the moment you walk into the room, the moment you approach the podium, or the moment you approach that individual. Nonverbal communications are sensitive to emotions and thoughts. Our thoughts are formed before our mind engages our will to perform our thoughts. So through nonverbal communications, a first impression may be formed.

When we meet someone for the very first time, the communication is instant. For example, when a speaker is introduced to an audience, the speaker is communicating with the audience nonverbally, before he or she speaks. When a sales representative is introduced to a customer, the sales person has communicated nonverbally through their dress, their facial expression, or body language even before he or she speaks with the customer. An impression is formed based on nonverbal communications such as posture, gesture, or eye contact. Have you ever noticed when you are introduced to someone, and before a word is spoken, the look in their eyes or facial expression says a lot?

For example, if your customer seems to be moving hastily, you might ask, "I know we planned an hour visit, but does that time period still work for you?"

If the customer tells you they have an urgent matter that requires their attention and can only spare five minutes for you, then express empathy and reschedule when you will be able to spend more quality time with the client. As things have changed on the customer's agenda, the customer would certainly appreciate your thoughtfulness.

On the other hand, the client may immediately connect with YOU and start to engage in small talk. This is good, because rapport is established. Stay alert and be prepared to transition to the selling stages. It is important that YOU maintain control while keeping the client engaged. It's all about selling YOU. And sometimes it's a balancing act.

You must communicate effectively to earn the right to advance. Always engage in active listening with the customer. It's amazing how much information the client will share with you, if you simply listen. Most clients like to talk about themselves or their business.

How many times have you met a client, started chatting, and before you knew it, gained valuable insight into them and their business? If that's happened, and you made the sale, it wasn't solely due to your service or business. What you sold was YOU!

In trusting YOU, the customer trusted your product or service, allowing you to win the business. Remember, there is only one first impression and it starts with YOU communicating effectively!

Demonstrate Great Listening Skills

The Free Dictionary defines listen as "to make an effort to hear something" or "to pay attention".

To communicate effectively, you must listen actively. Effective communication is when Party A's intended message equals Party B's perception of the same message.

Listening is the vital ingredient in communications. Practicing excellent listening skills can make a deal, and practicing poor listening skills can break a deal. Value the customer and value every single word they say!

Most new salespeople are taught a specific selling cycle with a standardized format. The format might include giving a product demonstration, a verbal or visual presentation. More experienced salespeople know to exercise flexibility with the use of the standard selling cycle. Once I started my own business I created my own strategy for selling. I discovered the best format is not necessarily a standard one. I get the customer to share information, to start talking and make sure I am actively listening. In listening, not talking, you are more apt to maintain control because you hear critical information that provides clues on how to close the customer and win the business!

Do you ever receive calls from telemarketers and once you say hello, they start selling you on a product, not knowing your needs? You want to tell them you already have a cell phone, or you just refinanced your home and have no need for additional services. Unfortunately, many telemarketers are trained to talk more than listen.

Have you ever tried to pour water into a cup that is full and the water overflows? Just as you cannot pour any more water into a full cup, your client is unable to speak, if you are doing all the talking. And when your client is not speaking, you are not gaining any new information to help progress the sales process or the relationship.

When you really want to obtain information from a customer, or any individual, there are three things you must do. Listen. Listen. Listen. During a sales call, the customer should speak the majority of the time and you should listen. When you think about what you want to accomplish during your sales meeting, you need to listen to the customer for any critical information that would enable your sale. For example, you might link the customer's goal or customer's need to your product or the benefits of your product. Listen and let the customer provide you with a reason that justifies your solution. When you listen to your customer you develop a strong partnership and the customer basically sells the solution for you through information sharing. Here are some listening facts:

- As adults, our listening is generally around 25% efficiency level.
- Over 50% of working hours are spent listening.
- People remember 50% of what is said after a 10 minute talk. Two days later they can only recall 25% of that same talk.
- 60% percent of management problems stem from ineffective listening skills.
- 70% to 90% of what an individual hears will be altered in their mind.
- Most Americans speak at a rate of 135 words per minute, but listen at a rate of 400 to 800 words per minute.

Let the customer know you are listening thru active listening. Nod to indicate agreement, question to clarify points, and leverage all the nonverbal signals through active listening. 93% of all communications is nonverbal. Listening, a nonverbal communications skill, has a huge impact in selling.

Make sure you are listening, not just hearing. Here's what I mean: *hearing* is mechanically or physically receiving sound via your ear. *Listening* is making a conscientious choice to receive sound via your ear and engage your brain to process the words from the sound to ensure your understanding of the content. Following are some tactics for listening.

Dos and Don'ts in Listening

Dos in Listening	Don'ts in Listening
Stay focused with eye contact	Be distracted
Capture content	Allow mind to wander
Be objective	Be subjective
Wait for pause, then ask question	Interrupt, unless clarification needed
Ask questions	Express inappropriate / no emotions
Summarize points	Engage in Selective Listening
Give feedback	Tune out
Listen to nonverbal body language	Cutoff speaker in middle of talk
Look for learning opportunities	Change context of what you hear

When listening, you have an opportunity to communicate nonverbally with the speaker. Nodding your head, along with eye contact, signals to the individual that you are tuned in and they have your undivided attention. Summarizing points or paraphrasing concepts tells the speaker the intended message equals the perceived message. In other words, you are really listening to understand what they are saying. For example, you might say, "If I understand you correctly the Department of Veteran Affairs needs additional staff for the CARE Project, but the freeze on hiring will not be lifted for 90 days. Is that right?"

Another essential part of listening is getting information to allow you to process the next step. Capturing the content will help you formulate the problem and solution. When you listen, note central points, key ideas, essential take-aways versus every word that is spoken.

Always work the person's name into your conversation. People like to feel important and hearing their name says they are important. How often have you been speaking to Deborah but calling her Demetria? I can remember misstating a customer's name early in my career and being immediately corrected. In fact, the customer interrupted my flow of communication to let me know their name. From that moment I have learned to discreetly write the name down, if necessary, at the beginning of our meeting. This way, I can always properly refer to the correct name as needed. The point is people want to hear you say their name. It shows that you listen well.

Be YOU!

In selling you, you must be interesting, knowledgeable, fun, listen well, and most of all, be YOU!

I remember once getting lost en route to a meeting with a new customer. I was only five minutes away, but I ended up calling the customer twice for additional directions, adding 30 minutes to my trip. I had to laugh at myself upon finally arriving at the customer location as I pictured myself riding around the same area for 30 minutes, not realizing the customer's location was within the same area. At the customer's office, I apologized and confessed about my terrible navigation skills. As I entered his office, I began to share my humor with my customer. I informed the customer that my sense of direction was an area for improvement.

I shared a story about my directional challenges. Once, I got lost driving around Washington, DC, I called a local friend for directions so many times that her husband answered the phone, not with a traditional "hello" greeting, but said: "Gloria, where are you now?"

I replied, "I am lost. I am in Baltimore, Maryland. Come get me now!" And to make matters even more senseless, I had a navigator in my car.

That story got a good laugh out of the customer and helped establish rapport. The point is, sometimes, to sell YOU is simply to be YOU. In selling in order to build the relationship, you have to reveal who you are.

The customer pleasantly smiled throughout my talk and even chuckled at times. When we started to discuss the customer's business needs, he offered valuable information to help me leverage my solution. In addition, the customer called in another key executive he wanted me to work with in formulating a solution for their business needs. From this meeting a cooperative and strong relationship commenced between the customer and me. Always know it's good to sell your strengths AND share your weaknesses. More importantly, always be YOU! Remember, in selling Start with YOU!

When we talk about Step #1 in selling, it Starts with YOU, I want you to think about this excerpt from the poem "You Tell on Yourself" by Harold Buckles:

> *"You tell on yourself by the friends you seek,*
> *by the very manner in which you speak.*
> *You tell what you are by the things you wear,*
> *by the spirit in which your burdens bear.*
> *You tell who you are by the way you walk,*
> *by the things of which you delight to talk."*

When we talk about successful selling, we are not talking about selling product, we are not talking about selling features, we are talking about selling YOU, and this applies for anything you are trying to sell or position. It all starts with YOU.

Step #2: Engage in Dialogue

Step #2: Engage in Dialogue is a critical step to selling. Today, we are more customer-focused than product-focused. This step should be a natural dialogue, not a monologue. You have to get the customer to talk in order to gain more insights about who they are, what they want, and why they really want it. Dialogue will give you more information on your audience.

Your objective is to better understand the customer's priorities, preferences, challenges and opportunities. How can you sell your product, service, or idea if you do not understand your audience; who they are, what they want, and why they want it?

It will be helpful to use the five Ws: (1) why, (2) what, (3) when, (4) where and (5) who. For example, you might ask the customer, "Why are we doing this? What time frame are you planning? Where will this take place?"

Lastly, throw in how and why, to ask open-ended questions. Open-ended questions keep your customer talking. Remember this stage is about dialogue, not monologue.

In the past, customers were willing to sit still and listen to the salesperson in the traditional telling sales approach, but today we live in an instant world, a *now* environment. The customer is more educated and has more choices. The salesperson must shift from being an expert to being a resource, a partner to the customer.

In the old days, the salesperson told a generic product story. You remember how the used car salesperson would approach the customer with Step One, "you want a car." Step Two, "I have the perfect car for you." Step Three, "Just step over here, let me show you this beautiful car, we'll get the paperwork complete, and you'll be cruising on the highway in minutes."

Today customers want more than the generic product story. Customers have more choices now. The customer wants to be engaged in the process from start to end. Customers want you to listen and understand their environment, their industry, trends, and needs. Customers want value, great customer service, and convenience. With dialogue selling, the *product story is blended with the customer story*, and the salesperson is a partner who listens.

So how do we begin dialogue? Well, Tom Hopkins, co-author of *The Certified Salesperson* says, "If I say it, they tend to doubt it. If they say it, it is true." So, allow the customer to talk and express their values. Let them say it.

But as a salesperson, you always need to be prepared to ask the right questions and maintain control. So, how exactly does this process work? Let's say you're in the door, past your greeting and introduction, and you're establishing rapport through small talk. This small talk could result from you acknowledging any recognition the customer might have received, i.e. Hospitality Partner of the Year Award. Or you might notice a New York Yankee team photo on the wall and briefly mention the Yankees winning the World Series.

From there you transition to the purpose of the call, give your agenda, and start with engaging in dialogue. You might start by asking the customer, "Tell me about your role in the organization and your key objective for the upcoming year." The point is, as a sales consultant, you must be prepared to initiate small talk to get the customer talking.

You will also position yourself as the student and your customer is the teacher. You want to learn, learn, and learn. People like you to be interested in what they have to say. Demonstrate active listening and total interest with your body language, your short responses like "I understand" or "Tell me more". You will be amazed at what the customer will share with you when you actively listen!

Your intention is to sell a specific product based on your initial phone conversation, but from actively listening to the customer, you may realize their product needs are different than what you assumed.

Say your customer prefers round bowls but you want to sell your surplus of square bowls. Rather than talk about the benefits of the square bowls or contradict the customer, ask, "Why do you prefer round bowls? Could you give me an example of how you plan to use the round bowls?"

The message here is to dig deep, to ask good questions that lead to dialogue. Dialogue leads to closing or winning the business.

Let's look at another scenario. You are selling personal computer solutions in the Services industry. You prepare to visit Ms. Jane Ellison, the Vice President of Operations for TimothyG Payroll Services, a company that provides payroll services to small and medium sized businesses in the United States. Ms. Ellison shares her frustration of spending too much money on overtime and not having enough money to upgrade all of the computers for the whole department. After further dialogue you convince Ms. Ellison that she could eliminate overtime expenses by upgrading hardware and software in the department. The savings from overtime elimination could be used to purchase a new personal computer solution from you, resulting in a win/win situation. Through engaging in dialogue with Ms. Ellison you are able to better understand the customer priority goals and the impact of the current environment in meeting the goals. By gaining insights into the hot button issues at TimothyG Payroll Services, you are able to link the value of your solution to your customer's real world concerns. When engaging in dialogue, you must remember to practice ABC, Always Be Closing.

Looking from a different angle, you may demonstrate value in your service versus value in a product. If you are selling a service, you might ask, what value the service brings to your customer? What value can you add to strengthen the relationship? And what about the customers who will not open up and give you information?

Some customers do not want to give you specific information. In this case, you ask them spin-off questions. A spin-off question is a question derived from a previously asked question, but asked in a different way.

For example, if you ask your customer, "What is the cost of your current service provider?" (original question)

They might say, "I'm not able to answer that question."

You later ask, "How much do you budget annually for service?" (spin-off question)

When they answer that, bingo! You now have an estimate of how much this customer pays their current service provider. Through effective use of a spin-off question you were able to obtain the same information indirectly.

Engaging in Dialogue is your opening ceremony like at the Olympics. Just remember, you cannot have a closing without an opening and **Step #2: Engage in Dialogue** is your grand opening.

At times I have observed sales people trying to sell without uncovering their customer's needs, and I can tell you this is a scene for daytime television. Let me share with you a story about Derek, skipping **Step #2: Engage in Dialogue** and **Step #3: Understand Customer Needs**, Derek began his sales talk in **Step #4: Position the Solution**. Derek started off at about 90 miles per hour pitching the value of his domestic auto parts to the owner of an auto dealership. He could have painted a picture, written a movie, and built a full size car from all the colorful illustrations he used during his sales presentation in efforts to position his solution. But when Derek asked for the order, the owner advised that the dealership only serviced *foreign* cars and they needed *foreign* parts, not domestic. The account call ended abruptly. Needless to say, Derek did not gain a relationship or get the deal. But hopefully he learned a lesson in selling.

How could Derek have avoided misreading the customer's needs? In the example, he did not get specific information about the customer's needs (information you would get during **Step #3: Understand Customer Needs**) because he did not probe the client with the right questions. How do you know what questions to ask during a sales call? Here is a hint: start with a basic open-ended question (a question you might ask during **Step #2: Engage in Dialogue**). For example you might ask, "What is the relationship with you current vendor like?" Or you might present it as a statement, "Tell me about your relationship with your current vendor."

From the customer's response, Derek will be able to confirm the type of product the customer's vendor sells (from his pre-call research on competition) and know the customer sells foreign auto parts only. From this information Derek will know to position his solution for a customer needing foreign auto parts.

Another pitfall is to avoid close-ended questions that can be answered with a simple yes or no, like, "Are you happy with your current computer vendor?"

Close-ended questions limit your opportunity to Engage in Dialogue. Close-ended questions work best in confirming or obtaining specific information.

Open-ended questions prompt the customer to speak longer while sharing their feelings, attitudes, and emotions in the process. Remember nonverbal communication is effective when you are engaging in dialogue with the customer. This step is early in the selling cycle, so you have an opportunity to observe the customer's facial expression, posture, and gestures, which allows you to respond accordingly. Also, when your customer speaks, you must show that you are engaged by using nonverbal cues like nodding, or adjusting your posture so you lean forward. Observing and participating in nonverbal communications is all a part of the selling cycle.

The verbal part of communications might occur face-to-face or via telephone. Verbal communications represent information received based on primary research, indicating you received the information directly from the source. Specifically, an open-ended question that you ask your client during a meeting is your on-site primary research, as you are receiving information directly from the source. Secondary research is information you obtain from another source and may not always be accurate or up to date. When you are able to gather information directly from the source, it is immensely beneficial.

An open-ended question answered live by the source provides first hand data and information, not second hand data and information. Close-ended questions lead to a specific answer. Lawyers use a lot of close ended questions when they want to lead the person to say specific words. Lawyers practice ABC, Always Be Closing. A closed-ended question often yields a yes or no response. Close-ended questions help guide the sales call so you can collect data, gain more insights, and verify the information prior to formulating your solution.

To assist you in how to start dialogue with customer, refer to the open-ended questions in table below. The most effective way to start the questioning with the customer is to ask broad questions, including a mix of high impact and open-ended questions. On the contrary, start asking the close-ended questions towards the end of your probing technique or to verify or qualify customer responses to high impact, open-ended questions.

Open-ended Questions	Closed-ended Questions
What are your top three goals for short term?	Is growth a major focus for you this year?
How do you plan to accomplish current year objectives?	Does your current plan include a budget to assist with goal attainment?
What do you need to accomplish your goals?	Are you planning to use external or internal trainers to facilitate professional development for your staff?

Open-ended Questions	Closed-ended Questions
Why is technology your biggest challenge?	Are competitive internet sales a threat to your market share?
Explain your decision making process.	Who is the ultimate decision maker for this project?
Tell me about your organizational objectives and your role to achieve them?	Are you responsible for supplier relationships along the value chain?

High Impact questions require preparation, research, and strategy. From your research and account call preparation, you will get more specific information about the customer to formulate high impact questions. High impact questions will yield a response from the customer that gives you a more complete and accurate picture of the company profile and company needs in which you will begin to position a solution. More importantly than generating responses that reflect a customer's assessment, emotion, opinion, and prediction, high impact questions provide you the right to advance to the next step in the sales call. Below are examples of high impact questions for use during **Step #2: Engage in Dialogue**:

➤ If we were able to provide a technology solution for your current issue, what would be the impact to your sales?

➤ Based on the current economic crisis, how has your competitive posture been challenged?

➤ With the use of automated technology at your point of sale, what is the impact to your value chain?

➤ With a downward economic trend last year and forecast for slight upward trend for next year, what is your "must have" going forward?

➤ If you had an opportunity to make a change for improvement, what would that change look like?

➢ With healthcare reform on the table, what is the projected impact for your medical facility's goals and objectives?

➢ With 20% missed forecast opportunities in the previous year, what plans are in place to achieve greater collaboration between sales game plan and operations allocation of resources?

➢ With the challenges facing mid level managers, how would it help your organization if we could improve communications within the entire leadership team?

➢ Given the current statistics noting a downward trend in new students, what specifically is not going well?

What happens when you find yourself searching for words to encourage the customer to talk more and give you more information? In other words, what do you do when the person does not have much to say or you are not getting the information you need to position a solution. If your customer is rambling, what step can you take to get the sales call back on track? Ask a question to lead the customer back to the subject matter or summarize pertinent information discussed up to this point. If the customer freezes up and does not want to answer your question, rephrase. Ask them what's most important to their organization's success? When the customer answers with a short or closed-ended response and you need more information, simply say, "Tell me more."

In essence, engaging in dialogue with a customer is like using a key to unlock a door of opportunity. Dialoguing with the customer opens the door to a wealth of information. You gain insights into the customer's environment, the customer's industry, the customer's competition, and customer's product or service. The next step is to gain confirmation on what the customer needs.

Step #3: Understand the Customer's Needs

At this stage you have sold yourself (**Step #1: Start with YOU**). You have gained knowledge and insights into the organizational environment (**Step #2: Engage in Dialogue**). Now you are ready to transition to **Step #3: Understand the Customer's Needs**. In this stage, you are summarizing information gathered in the previous steps to size up your opportunity, verify the customer needs, and qualify the customer. You want to ensure your understanding of the customer's needs, and do final probing to uncover any additional needs or customer "must haves" and "don't wants".

This is the gut of your call. If this is not clearly identified, there is no reason to move on. You must identify and verify the customer's needs in this stage and you must summarize their needs to demonstrate your understanding.

Many times customers do not even know what they need. As a resource, expert, and partner, you should ask questions to identify the real need. As a professional salesperson, your objective is to distinguish between implied needs and explicit needs. Implied needs express customer displeasure about a situation, but do not necessarily warrant an immediate solution to fix the problem. An example of an implied need is when a customer comments, "I am so unhappy with the speed of our current computer system."

On the other hand, explicit needs shout out for an immediate solution. The problem has proven costly to the customer who feels the value of the solution far outweighs the cost of the current problem. An example of an explicit need is, "We need a faster system to allow us to compete in the global market."

You might want to create a "cheat sheet" of questions to ask. More specific questions are asked during this step to verify the customer needs. In **Step #2: Engage in Dialogue**, you might want to start with more high impact, open-ended questions to demonstrate your knowledge of the customer environment. In **Step #3: Understand the Customer's Needs**, you may incorporate a lower impact approach, but still ask open-ended questions until you feel you have a complete understanding of the customer needs. Here are some more suggested open-ended questions and statements:

- ➤ Please tell me about your organization and your role.
- ➤ How do you like your current supplier of training materials?
- ➤ What do you want to accomplish first?
- ➤ What do you need to do to accomplish that goal?
- ➤ How do you measure the effectiveness of goal attainment?
- ➤ Tell me more.
- ➤ How would you describe your relationship with your current supplier?
- ➤ Why is management morale low?
- ➤ What three objectives must you accomplish this year?
- ➤ What gives your organization the competitive edge?
- ➤ How will the success of this project be measured?

Today, we operate in a knowledge-based environment. You must conduct research to gain insight about your customer prior to meeting with the customer. Obtaining appropriate knowledge during the opening steps of the selling cycle is weighted heavier than closing in the selling process, because when you do the appropriate work on the front end, the back end is easy. In other words, the close requires less effort when you have a clear understanding of the customer's environment and needs. Yogi Berra, famed New York Yankee player, once stated, "If you do not know where you are going, you will end up someplace else."

I would like to add the following, "If you do not know where you are going, you will NEVER get there." In order to Position Your Solution and close the sale, you must know your customer's needs, continue to dialogue, and earn the right to advance through the stages of selling.

Be prepared to increase the customer's awareness of their needs. Through proper research and probing, you will gain information that allows you to close the gap between the customer's needs and your solution. A customer may tell you they need to train their management staff to better motivate their employees. As you begin to ask questions, you uncover negative issues that correlate more with subordinates than managers. Low morale and employee dissatisfaction is surfacing. Managers are constantly trying to shift subordinates' attitude from negative to positive with little success. Upon further probing, the customer and you agree that providing training for the subordinates, instead of management, will better address their needs. In better understanding the customer, employee skill development emerges as the critical need and way to incent the employees to exercise self-motivation while enriching their skills in the work environment.

Once you have a conceptual view of the customer's needs, ask more close-ended questions to confirm your understanding. Here are some more closed-ended questions:

➢ Have you considered providing training materials for each participant to reinforce their learning?
➢ Is it safe to say you are seeking a quicker way to prepare invoices?
➢ Will you be the person to make the final decision regarding the recommendation?

> ➢ Are you prepared to move forward with the implementation this year?
> ➢ Are you saying you need a more efficient way to process the gift basket orders during peak season?
> ➢ May we confirm a meeting for next Friday?
> ➢ What time-frame do you have in mind?
> ➢ Do you have a budget allocated for this program?
> ➢ Are you the sole decision maker for this project?
> ➢ How many computers do you currently have for your sales team?

During this process, you are summarizing and verifying customer needs. You might say, "You stated your current computer system is outdated compared to competition. Is that correct?"

Never advance to **Step #4: Position Your Solution** prior to verifying and prioritizing customer needs. And in clarifying, keep the tone conversational. You are building a relationship, not a debate team. You want to partner with the customer, not compete with the customer. Be sensitive to the customer's tone. Listen for what they say…and what they don't say. Know clearly and completely what the customer's needs—not desires—are. Confirm the customer's priorities for the current year objectives. For example, if a customer has expressed a need for three training modules, but has a budget that only allows for one training module, clearly identify the 'must have' training module and the current budget allocation.

Lastly, ensure the customer and you are in agreement with the needs and the priorities of the needs before you even think about moving to **Step #4: Position Your Solution**. You want to summarize the customer's needs and tie the needs to their goals in the process. Check-in with the customer along the way to ensure you have assessed their needs correctly.

So many times the customer shares a *perceived* need, not a *real* need. As a consultant and for clarification purposes, your job is to transition the perceived need to a real need. For example, the customer might say, "We need more time in a workday and additional personnel to take physical inventory to ensure we are always able to meet demand."

Your response, "What I hear you saying is that you need a more efficient way to manage inventory. Is that a fair statement?"

The customer may simply need to automate some aspect of the physical inventory, versus a need for more people or more time in a workday. Here are some additional qualifying and clarifying questions:

- ➢ How are they currently scheduling meetings?
- ➢ What is the current square footage of your home?
- ➢ How many orders do you process a day?
- ➢ How many students do you need to enroll to reach growth goal?
- ➢ Why is that important?
- ➢ If I understand you correctly, you need a way to improve the process...is that correct?
- ➢ I would like to recommend a program that will address your needs. Who will make a decision to move forward on the recommendation and in what time-frame?
- ➢ If I can demonstrate a program that will improve communications within your organization, will you commit to the recommendation?
- ➢ Will you be willing to move forward with a program that would include a sample population of your organization at this time?
- ➢ "Ms. Watson, from my understanding, you are most interested in a system that will allow you to track revenue from all your real estate properties in a timely manner. This system will enable you to attain your goal of minimizing or eliminating bad debt. Is this a correct summary?"
- ➢ Are there any other items you would like to add at this time?

In verifying and qualifying your customer needs, you want to ensure clarity in the dialogue exchange. Appropriately leveraging transition statements are encouraged. While transition statements are not substitutes for the core message, transition statements can complement and help to clarify the message. The following are examples of transition statements:

> ➢ Let's bring it all together and see how our team building solution will yield Wicker Incorporated a high performance team.

> ➢ In lieu of this global change, you might want to consider updating technology. Let's look at some options.

> ➢ While your current operations are adequate for the current product line, let's look at expanding operations to accommodate your new growth plan.

If you are pushed for time or not prepared for a lot of questioning, always have one key question in mind. For example, "What are your expectations for any trainer you hire to provide leadership training?"

Good qualifying questions work both professionally and personally. On a personal level, when I interviewed for sales jobs and was asked at the end of the interview if I had any questions, I would always ask two questions:

> ➢ **Can you describe a day in the life of your #1 salesperson?** Based on their response, I would follow up with a statement and example demonstrating my ability to be that #1 salesperson.

> ➢ **If you were interrupted during this meeting with an urgent message from your boss to make a decision**

immediately on your candidate of choice, would I be that person? If they said yes, I would graciously thank them and close with, "I am looking forward to being a major contributor to this high performance team at XZY Company."

If they said "no" or "I don't know", I would probe for more information. The important thing is this: if you do not ask the right questions, you will never get the right answers. And if you do not get the right answers, you will not position the right solution nor win the business.

In addition to summarizing and verifying needs, customers must be qualified for funds availability. A qualified customer is one that has a need, has an interest in a solution to the need, and has a budget to pay for a solution to the need. If the customer does not have any money, you do not have a sale. Customers must be qualified for timeline and implementation process. If the customer is qualified to move forward with a timeline for implementation, you will be able to successfully coordinate the supply and install process. Qualifying a customer for budget allocation will tell you if a customer is able to buy now or must delay until next year. A qualifying question might ask, "If I can show you a solution for your skills gap, are you prepared to move forward with implementation?"

The difference between a good salesperson and a great salesperson is qualifying prospects and selling to a pool of high *quality* prospects versus a pool of high *quantity* prospects.

Appropriate questions to qualify customer must be asked during this stage. Example: "If I find you a three-bedroom home with a $2000 monthly mortgage, will you purchase the home?"

Or, "If I identify an internal networking system that will eliminate your overtime in the Information Technology Department, will you install the solution?"

If the customer is qualified to purchase, then you are qualified to move to **Step #4: Position Your Solution**.

Step #4: Position Your Solution

In real estate it's all about location, location, location. In selling it's all about position, position, position. This is the new lingo for 21st century selling. You no longer present your products. You no longer present your services. Today you Position Your Solution. Positioning your solution means sharing your recommendation from your *customer's* point of view. Presenting your solution means sharing your recommendation from *your* point of view, which isn't what you want to do?

When you Position Your Solution, you want the customer to feel it, taste it, smell it, and see themselves using your product. You want your client to see the value and realize the benefit of your solution. Once you have the customer using the product, the sale is virtually closed. So, how do we get the buyer to mentally buy-in and realize the implementation of your solution? Position. Position. Position.

In positioning your products and service, you want to build upon what you have learned. For example, after I probed and probed to understand a customer's environment, I positioned three potential solutions (solutions A , B, and C) by linking the customer's needs to the benefit of each of the solutions. While my goal was to sell one of three options, I positioned three options to demonstrate added value.

While proceeding to gain the customer's agreement on the first option, Solution A, the customer readily indicated she liked Solution

B. The customer informed me she could see Solution B working successfully within her organization. Upon hearing the three solutions, the customer visualized Solution B successfully working to solve the company operational problems. Solution B updated technology along the supply chain, thus improving productivity and customer service. So, we went with Solution B. I looked the customer in the eye once I realized there was a relationship link. There was a bridge from my solution to the customer's needs. I closed the deal and went into the next step to implement the solution.

Consultative selling is cooperative selling. The buyer participates in the process with the seller, step-by-step. By the time you reach **Step #4: Position Your Solution**, the buyer has a mental picture of the solution and is beginning to visualize the benefits. In this stage of selling, you want to present a clear path that answers the WIFM (What's In It For Me?) for the customer.

When you Position Your Solution, you must always move the customer towards a yes. When we talk about positioning our product, service, or idea, we talk about linking our features and benefits, not presenting them. We all know features are elements of the product. Features build credibility.

Shaquille O'Neal built credibility with the Los Angeles Lakers when they were winning in the early 2000's. The local ads would say, "Come see the Los Angeles Lakers, FEATURING Shaquille O'Neal." When Shaquille left the Lakers organization and the team lost more games the following year, the credibility diminished. Ticket sales went down the year after Shaq was traded to the Miami Heat. Features build credibility.

Benefits are what the customer gains from the elements of the product. Benefits answer the WIFM. Benefits promote marketability.

Tiger Woods is a benefit to the Professional Golf Association. When Tiger plays, ratings soar, promoting marketability. Roger Federer is a benefit to the International Tennis Association. David Beckam is a benefit to the world of soccer. You get the picture.

What is the benefit of your product or service to the customer? What features of your service plan build credibility for your establishment? These are questions you answer in the selling cycle when you Position Your Solution from the customer's point of view.

When I sold computers I never focused solely on computer features because customers had so many choices among competing products. I always positioned the total solution offering, not just computer features. I always based the solution on the customer needs.

For example, if the customer was concerned with quality, I positioned the quality of our brand. If the customer wanted the right price, I positioned the price as "all-inclusive". If the customer wanted value, I positioned "value pricing". If the customer needs reflect exclusiveness, I positioned "premium pricing", and so on...

My favorite fragrance is Clive Christian perfume. This perfume was initially sold exclusively at Neiman Marcus. The exclusivity could have originally been a credible feature for Neiman Marcus and the perfume manufacturer. Some people buy things to be the exclusive owner. The key is if the customer's need reflects exclusiveness, Position Your Solution as "exclusive". If the customer's need reflect value, Position Your Solution as "value priced". Remember, positioning is based on what the customer wants or needs.

The key difference between presenting your product and positioning your product is this third and critical part to the formula, the customer's story. The customer's story is told during **Step #2: Engage in Dialogue**, and by linking the customer's story to your features and benefits, you have not only positioned your products and services, but you have customized the solution based on the customer's point of view.

Position Your Solution is one of my favorite parts of selling. I have an opportunity to help an individual or organization succeed through my product or service. This is a step I must control in the process. How do you control this step?

First, you must visualize the sale. You must see the customer enjoying the benefits of your solution so that you may articulate those benefits in laying out the solution. Success is generated from the inside out. If you see and feel the success, the customer will as well. When you look at the greatest athletes' achievements, their best games come out of the worst situations. Winners dig deep to succeed. Winners plant seeds to succeed. Winners believe they will succeed. In selling, you must believe it and visualize it first, only then can you Position Your Solution.

You must always keep the customer involved and interactive in the process. You might ask the customer, "Do you see how this service will be helpful to your leadership team?" Or, "What additional value do you see yourself receiving from this technology update?" In other words, you want to know if you are hitting a home run or if you are stuck on third base and need to demonstrate more value or additional benefits.

Finally, bring it all together with the benefit to the customer. You might comment, "We just viewed a technology platform that will enable XYZ Company productivity and improve customer satisfaction. Did you see how impactful this platform will be to your company growth?" The key is to keep the customer saying yes as you progress through the selling stages.

Positioning your solution should be the climax of the meeting. You want this process to showcase the best of the best: YOU, and your product! Remember, how the Los Angeles Lakers Team of the 80's would advertise, "Come see the Lakers, Showtime." Why? Because the Lakers Basketball Team of the 80's put on a show for the audience. As buyers, we rush to purchase tickets for events that we visualize as exciting and entertaining. People visualize Disneyland as exciting and entertaining! Tickets sell easily. President Obama's inauguration was exciting and entertaining! Inauguration Ball tickets sold easily! In this stage, you have an opportunity to make your solution exciting, interesting, and a "must have"! If you succeed, your product or service will sell easily!

As a seller you must be enthusiastic and passionate about your product. If you are, your customer will want that enthusiasm and passion as well! Everybody wants to share in the good!

Be cautioned, though. At this stage you want the sale. You are not trying to establish rapport. You are trying to position yourself to win the business. Do not allow your enthusiasm to lead you to overselling the customer in this step. Here is when you are beginning to transition to the next Step #5: The Close, and you do not want to get overexcited at this point and start promising things you cannot deliver. If you revert to a different character dynamic, like extreme enthusiasm, all of a sudden, you risk appearing phony at this stage. Your enthusiasm should Start with YOU in the first stage of selling and carry you throughout the process.

While you may be highly passionate about the product, you do not want your enthusiasm to overshadow the benefits of the product. Strike the right balance with the right audience. It's good to share critical points in threes. You might state, "With the use of wireless technology throughout your sales organization, you can quickly correspond with anyone across the globe. Secondly, with wireless technology your Sales and Operations teams may better collaborate to ensure accurate resources are allocated for all locations. Lastly, wireless technology will improve productivity throughout your organization and enhance customer activity."

Keep the talk relevant to the solution at hand. Customers may access other details through leave-behind literature, websites, or other miscellaneous sales materials. Because some research studies suggest a human's average attention span is eight seconds, you must focus on key points only in this stage. To keep the buyer's mind focused on visualizing the solution, communicate clear and concise information so you do not overcrowd the picture.

It's helpful to position external references during this stage. For example you might share that, "ABC Company implemented this platform earlier this year and has enjoyed benefits in productivity and cost."

Be prepared and confident enough so that when you share customer reference information, you may also share reference contact information, should your buyer want to contact the customer to confirm value. When selling within a vertical industry, you may have to exercise sensitivity due to competitive nature. But when selling across industries, leveraging external references is extremely resourceful.

I often acquire new customers through references from my existing customer base due to the relationship and value of my service. As a buyer myself, when I go into a store to purchase a particular outfit for a specific occasion, if the representative that I normally do business with is unable to fit me in an outfit of my needs, she happily refers me to an appropriate store that will satisfy my attire needs. Yet I will always go to my regular representative first and give her an opportunity for the sale because she always handles my needs directly or indirectly. In the Position Your Solution stage, sometimes the solution may be to partner with an external company. While you may lose the sale this time, you will gain a lifelong satisfied customer! In selling, the customer's needs are always the priority.

"How to Say It" Tactics

How you say it may be more impactful than *what* you say during the Position Your Solution stage. Here are some "How to Say It" tactics to assist you in the process:

> ➤ Speak in plain, everyday English. Do not try to impress with big words that do not fit the setting.

> ➤ Speak it like you really mean it! Remember, you must believe in the solution first, convincing your customer is second.

> ➤ Speak in second person so the customer may visualize the actual solution working to his or her advantage. For instance, "The next couple of slides will focus on the key benefits we agreed are critical to your team's success."

➤ Share the features of your solution and clearly articulate the solution, so that the customer will quickly grasp how it will help them with their needs.

➤ Review the advantages of your solution by linking the benefits to the customer needs.

During the Position Your Solution stage your main objective is to provide a solution that the customer will agree to implement. You will give an overview of the solution and the solution advantage, linking the customer needs. You will speak to the features, and how the features relate to the customer's needs in an effort to gain their business.

Features build credibility, benefits promote marketability, but positioning delivers the deal. Before you move to the fifth and final step, let's talk about objections.

Objections

Yes, you will get objections. Objections are opportunities to address obstacles. When customers present obstacles it indicates interest; they simply want more information to progress the sale. Objections mean the customer is turned on and is interested in your positioning but simply need some answers. If the customer was not interested, you would not have made it to this stage. Customers present objections in a variety of ways. Your job is to accurately interpret and answer the objection.

How do you deal with objections? Do you say, "Heck, I don't need this hassle," and graciously terminate the meeting with the customer? Do you freeze up because the customer is screaming at you? Do you answer the objection completely with integrity and honesty?

Always answer the objection completely with integrity and honesty. Please do not lie to the customer! Let me share a quote from Spencer Johnson, author of *One Minute Manager* and *Who Moved My Cheese,* which distinguishes these two elements of truth, "Integrity is telling yourself the truth and honesty is telling the truth to other people."

During the objection process, you want to acknowledge the objection and demonstrate empathy prior to answering the objection. For instance, you might state, "I clearly hear what you are saying and I understand why you might feel that way. But let me share with you some recent success we experienced with Columbia Realty Management who expressed similar concerns."

Proceed to share the similar scenario to either minimize or reverse the customer's objection. And prior to progressing to the next stage in the selling cycle, confirm that you have answered or satisfied the customer's concern.

Objection may be another way a customer will ask for more information. For example, a customer might say, "I don't see this platform working in our environment."

The interpretation of this statement is, "Please provide additional information on how this platform will work in our environment."

Objection may be presented as a cover up. The customer may not have the money to pay for the solution, but may say, "I do not think your solution is a good fit for our company."

At this point you want to probe further to completely understand what "not a good fit" means. In further probing you discover the customer does not have the funding to support the solution. You ask, "Are you saying your current year's budget will not accommodate this solution?"

If the customer is unable to fund your solution this year, gain agreement on when future funding will be available.

Empathize with the customer's objection, but never agree with the objection. Remember you have to always believe in your solution before you can get your customer buy-in. Here are some empathizing statements for handling objections:

> I understand how you feel. ABC Company felt the same way at first, but four weeks after implementation, they found the benefits far outweighed their initial concerns.

> I appreciate your concern. Let's look at an alternative option. If we consider implementing the solution in two phases, your current year budget will support Phase I and we will

implement Phase II once you have confirmed next year's budget.

> Help me understand your concern regarding availability of personnel to commit to the project right now. What exactly do you mean when you say you do not have the personnel? I appreciate your concern. XYZ Company felt the same way initially, but found out the solution actually enhanced personnel productivity.

> SanDawna, I recognize your need for more time. What date may we schedule to speak further regarding the solution and what additional information might Speaking Essentials provide to help you in the process?

Objections should be viewed as an opportunity. Objections mean the customer is turned on, not off. Objections are questions that need answers. An objection is the one item that stands before closing the sale. Objections will be minimized if appropriate information is shared and agreed upon throughout the selling process.

As a sales representative, if you are hearing the same objections with all clients, I suggest you rework your sales pitch. Ensure you have thoroughly researched the customer information, so you can answer questions completely and accurately, leaving no gaps for objections. Have some statistics on hand to quantify your solution and add value as to how you respond to objections. Some clients make decisions based on analyzing information; numbers will help them see the benefits clearer.

Once, I had a client that really liked my solution, but felt cost would negatively impact the decision. From my research, I knew the client was launching a new mentoring program that would measure results of students who were assigned mentors versus students who were not assigned mentors. The client agreed my solution would benefit the mentoring program, but cost was an issue. I suggested implementing the solution for a sample population and comparing results of individuals from the sample population who used the solution versus individuals who did not use the solution.

Always demonstrate confidence when handling objections. Confidence allows you to overcome any difficulties you might encounter. I remember preparing a PowerPoint presentation to position my solution to a client. Before I could sit down, the customer handed me an objection, "Gloria, do not present a PowerPoint to me. I do not want to see a PowerPoint. I just want you to tell me why I should give my business to you."

These are times when you really, really need your confidence. I was ready. I always come to my clients with confidence, knowledge, flexibility, and a positive attitude. I looked this particular client in the eye and gave three benefits they would gain from doing business with my company: (1) expand customer base, (2) grow sales, and (3) increase brand awareness. And I gave additional support information to justify each one of the benefits.

On the other hand you may experience Objections early in the selling cycle. Will you have customers that refuse to speak with you when you call? Yes. What is your next step in this situation? It depends. If the customer is adamant about you not calling again, do not call again. Never get into a conflict with a customer. The result could be costly and irreparable.

If a customer refuses to speak with you *at this time*, you might want to keep their name on your Mail Only list. Send a Christmas card, sample product, or industry literature to stay in touch. Eventually, the customer may stop objecting and speak with you.

Once you have answered the objection and gained customer agreement, you have earned the right to advance to the final step in successful selling, **Step #5: The Close**.

Step #5: The Close

S tep 5: The Close, this is the win, when you bring it all home, the grand finale. You have to ask for the sale or ask for agreement to move forward with your positioned product, service, or idea here.

The worst move a salesperson can make is to energize the customer, get them excited about their solution, then leave the customer's office having never asked for the order.

In business, *never* assume, *always* ask for the order. When you have successfully executed steps 1 - 4, and answered all objections completely with honesty and integrity, the closing is automatic.

Closing Techniques

Here are some closing techniques to use when asking for the order or when gaining agreement on your recommendation:

➤ **Fundamental Closing** – Make assumption. Which area of the house would you like to start on first?

➤ **Alternative Closing** – Give choice. Would you like the ivory or pink towels for the guest bathroom?

➢ **Impeding Event Closing** – Notate urgency. Would you like to start with the roof project next week so when the rainy season arrives the job will be complete?

➢ **Puppy Dog Closing** – Give trial product or service. Ask prospect to try the product or service for a given period of time with no obligation. For example, give a 90-day subscription for access to monthly credit reports or get People Magazine FREE for first 90 days.

Closing is what separates the winners from the losers. The top 20% of salespeople will close sales 80% of the time. Engaging in dialogue, understanding the customer needs, and positioning the solution does not matter if you do not close the sale. You must lead the customer to the close. Customers rely on your expertise and consultative skills to provide guidance on the best solution for their needs. In speaking with clients about training or speaking needs, my first priority is to gather the necessary information through research and probing. My second priority is to build the relationship and win the sale in the process. If I lose the sale during my first attempt, I continue to strengthen the relationship and eventually get the sale and continue to deepen the relationship.

When I won Area Sales Representative of the Year with Pitney Bowes Corporation, my strategy was to work hard, not smart. In prior years I was successful in gaining lots of small sales resulting in my exceeding the annual sales quota. In my award year, I sought a different approach. My tactics were risky, but rewarding. I passed a lot of small sales to other representatives in order to focus on building relationships with bigger sales prospects. And it worked! In one case I actually closed the sale during the last day of the year and that sale put me at 270% of quota for the month and 142% of quota for the year.

Had I not been persistent to get that huge sale the last day of the year, I would not have made quota. Had I not asked for the order, I would not have won the business. In fact, the customer had put a Do Not Disturb sign on the door, noting they were closed due to year-end processing. Because I had already built a relationship, I was able to get through that barrier to meet with my customer. Because I started with me and built a relationship in selling, I won the business and the relationship!

Good salespeople close sales; great salespeople close relationships. When you close the relationship you establish trust and respect between the customer and you. When you close the relationship, the customer will begin to seek you as a resource and partner.

I once worked with an individual who was outstanding in closing sales. Because she never took the time to close the customer on a relationship, she never kept a sales job. She often asked if I would be a reference for her to get a sales job with a new company. This mentality is equated to winning the battle, but losing the war. Selling in the 21st century is built on relationship and partnering, not closing one-on-one sales.

Closing a sale is automatic when probing is done effectively. When you have the knowledge and the history, you are better equipped to deal with what's to come. It's like going to work with a new personal trainer. Until the new trainer is acquainted with your history, little progress is made. The success in closing a sale stems from the support information gathered upfront in **Step #2: Understand Customer Needs** and **Step #3: Engage in Dialogue**.

When closing a sale, you might want to wait to exhale. Wait for the customer to respond to your question. Silence is key to hearing what the customer has to say at this point. You want to be actively listening so that you hear the customer say yes.

At times you may be able to close the sale during an earlier phase of selling. Always be flexible and prepared. Remember, nonverbal communication represents 93% of all communications. Stay tuned in to the customer's body language. Always listen objectively. In **Step #3: Engage in Dialogue**, the customer may hint that they are very interested in your solution. For example, the customer might say, "Are the assessments included in the Leadership Training Program?" Or, "Would you be able to train my staff on the computer software?" Actively listen to your customer and respond to the clues they give you so you can close the sale early in the cycle, when appropriate.

During **Step #5: The Close**, you always want to highlight key benefits because, once again, the average attention span is eight seconds. Here are some additional facts as to why restating your solution will help the customer during this step, according to research by National Science Foundation as noted in Charlie Greer's article "*What Are You Thinking?*":

➢ During a day, a deep thinker thinks approximately 45,000 thoughts

➢ During a day, an average thinker thinks approximately 12,000 thoughts

➢ During an hour, majority of individuals think 1000 thoughts

➢ Within a minute, majority of individuals think approximately 20 thoughts

➢ Within three seconds, majority of individuals think approximately one thought

These statistics demonstrate why you should take a few minutes to review solution benefits prior to asking for the business. This review will enable the customer to focus on the WIFM, What's In It for Me?

Here's an example: "Charlene you stated a need to have the individual staff members think more in terms of one team. We discussed Speaking Essentials' "Team Building to Win" presentation includes interactive exercises to reinforce theories and bring individuals together as a team. Jean you stated a need to improve productivity. We discussed updating technology along the supply chain."

In reviewing the benefits, you are positioning value in the customer's mind and planting seeds of success. The cost of the solution is minimized while the value is optimized in the process.

Once you have won the business, it is equally important that you put forth the effort to maintain the customer. Research tells us it will cost you five times as much to acquire a new customer versus maintaining the existing customer. The Pareto 80/20 rule might conclude 80 percent of your business will come from 20 percent of your customer base. Remember you want to win the relationship, not just the sale. So get started…Start with YOU!

Closing a sale is a cooperative and exciting phase for all parties. Closing yields a win/win situation when steps 1- 4 of selling are effectively executed. Whether you are closing on an idea, a service, or product, you must demonstrate confidence that you have earned the right to be there. You must ensure all challenges have been responded to completely and honestly before you get to the Closing. As a salesperson, you should take the lead, but you want your buyer to actively participate. Ensure all decision-making parties are engaged in the process during Closing. During this stage, be prepared to collaborate or compromise to win the sale. Know in advance your negotiation strategy. Whenever the customer has agreed to your solution or any benefit, ask your customer, "Are you prepared to move forward with this plan at this time?"

Remember the Listening Technique. Wait to exhale and listen, listen, listen. Should you have to negotiate, Position Your Solution in response to the customer's previous agreement on a benefit. For example, you might say, "I understand your staff lacks technical skills and will require training. Do you agree the new technology will handle your greater problem of speed and increased sales?"

And if the customer says yes, the next step is for you to negotiate on training the staff. Your company may want to offer training for half of the customer's staff. Your company may want to offer a "Train the Trainer" program, wherein you train one or two individuals from the company and *they* will be responsible for training others in their company. The key is being prepared to effectively negotiate during the closing stage.

Once all negotiations are agreed upon, a decision has been made, and you have closed the sale, it's important to discuss the next step, the Action Plan.

Action Plan

Once you have gained the customer's agreement and closed the sale, an action plan must be established to implement the solution. You and the customer need to agree on upcoming activities and timelines as well as identify the responsible parties who will perform the activities. Always follow-up with the customer 60 to 90 days after your solution is implemented to gather any feedback or measurement of results. When you follow-up with your client, you have an opportunity to deepen the relationship as well as gain more business. Once you have sold the customer, servicing the customer begins. Whether it is through monitoring implementation of the solution, or communications with your customer regarding future needs, servicing is an opportunity for you to differentiate your brand from competition. Servicing is an opportunity for you to recycle the process and gain a very satisfied customer, a referral, or more business from the same customer.

To illustrate the focus of the five steps to successful selling is a poem below:

Start with YOU

Start with YOU!
That's the cue.
Engage in Dialogue,
Not Monologue.
Understand the Customer Needs
It helps to Plant the Seeds.
Position Your Solution
For the Evolution.
Handle the Objection
With Truthful Passion.
Ask for the commitment
During the Closing Session.
And ...Remember, it all Starts with YOU!

While selling is an art that requires discipline, commitment, and risk, the rewards are both professionally and personally gratifying. Selling is professionally gratifying when you help others achieve their goals, and they value you! Selling is personally gratifying when you help others achieve their goals, and you win the relationship! As previously stated, people buy from you if they like you. People like you if they trust you and respect you. Just remember in selling, it all Starts with YOU!

A Day on Selling Something Street

I want you to imagine you are a salesperson given a challenging territory with a diverse set of customers on Selling Something Street who has completed Sales Course titled, *How to Sell YOU...and Your Product, Service, or Idea.*

As you are driving on Selling Something Street, you will confidently face up to a difficult customer situation and make the best of it demonstrating heroism. You will earn your Outstanding Rescue medal as you Engage in Dialogue and recover a sale from a position where it could have been lost.

You are to be applauded because when things went wrong, you didn't go with them. You are to be commended for recovering a potential lost sale. You stuck it out to win. "Oh my, you've earned more," a firefighter gold medal. You have just calmed the flames of an upset customer after listening to the customer express all their concerns. And lastly, your management team commends you on this day as you are pulled from the bottom of the well. You took that customer from a position of no interest to acquisition of interest in your custom-tailored solution. You won the business!

Congratulations in demonstrating successful selling while driving on Selling Something Street. You Engaged in Dialogue. You Understood the Customer's Needs. You Positioned Your Solution. You Closed the Sale. And remember, it all Started with YOU! Now you have the necessary tools to engage in successful selling. Now you have the necessary tools to win the relationship and the sale! Start with YOU...that's the Cue!

About the Author

Gloria Wadsworth is a Motivational Speaker and Trainer. She is the CEO/President of Speaking Essentials INC. With a strong background in Organizational Management Development, Gloria partners with individuals and businesses to deliver strategic team and individual-performance building projects to assist them in achieving their goals and objectives.

Gloria has 30 years of business experience with Fortune 100 Companies like IBM, Pitney Bowes, and American Express. She is a University of Phoenix Faculty Member and adjunct faculty member at National University. Gloria is a Certified Trainer of DiSC®, a behavioral assessment to help individuals better understand themselves and others. In 1992 she was Area Sales Representative of the Year for Pitney Bowes Corporation.

She has a Masters of Arts in Organizational Management from the University of Phoenix and a Bachelors of Science in Business Administration from the University of South Carolina.

Gloria is a member of Faithful Central Bible Church (FCBC) in Los Angeles where she serves on the Deaconess Ministry and is an instructor in the Champions in Training program at FCBC.

Growing up in a Christian culture, Gloria developed a very strong and personal relationship with God. From this relationship she has learned that no matter what happens in life these two things are infinite and eternal: God's love for her, and her love for God.

Booking Information

To book Gloria Wadsworth for a speaking or training engagement or for more information about any of Speaking Essentials INC training programs or products, contact us:

Speaking Essentials INC
PO Box 91332
Los Angeles CA 90009

Phone: 310 527 2511
Email: wadsworthg@sbcglobal.net
Visit our Website: www.speakingessentials.com

"DiSC®", "Everything DiSC®", and "Inscape Publishing®" are registered trademarks of Inscape Publishing, Inc. Used with permission. All rights reserved.

To help you sell YOU... Take DiSC® Classic 2.0 (online assessment) and learn your individual behavioral tendencies in communications, relationships, and conflict.

Call 310 527 2511 to order the DiSC assessment, mention the book *How to Sell YOU...and Your Product, Service, or Idea* and receive a $10 savings. The assessment report will be sent to you via email and your results will be forwarded to your email upon completion.